THE CREATOR'S HANDBOOK

SHINGAI SAMUDZI

Copyright © 2022

All Rights Reserved. No part(s) of this book may be reproduced, distributed or transmitted in any form, or by any means, or stored in a database or retrieval systems without prior expressed written permission of the author of this book.

Acknowledgements

To my parents, for creating a home environment without ideological or historical constraints.

Contents

Acknowledgements iii

Introduction 1

The Foundation 7
    Breath 7
    From Breath to Flow 11

Part 1: The Right Frame of Mind 15
    Mindset 15
    Visualizing the Future 16
    Describing the Future in a Tangible Way 20
    Goals vs. Strategy vs. Tactics 23
    Implementing Tactics 24
    Failure 27
    Success 27
    Myth of the Orderly Universe 29
    Ends vs. Means 31
    Context and Zeitgeist 31

Luck 32

Probability 33

First Hand vs. Second Hand information 35

Principles for Taking Action 37

Research and Avoiding Surprise............................37

Part 2: Working with others 39

Bias - The Decision-making Toolkit 41

Ego and the Individual 45

Utility Monsters 46

The Role of Worldviews in Shaping Behavior 50

Cognitive Dissonance 53

The Unconscious Mind...54

Mechanics of Influence...56

Indirect Triggers 57

Pull techniques 58

Push Techniques..59

Debate 61

Swaying the Marginalized 61

Swaying the Zealots 62

Managing Uncertainty..63

Part 3: Group Level 65

Foundations of a Network 65

The Human Machine 68

Degrees of Separation 69

Tactical Resources 70

Communicating Push 70

Managing Networks or Organizations 71

Network composition 71

Weak versus Strong Bonds 72

Structure 74

Cost of Information Sharing 75

Diversity of Perspective 78

Trust and Violence 80

Network Maintenance 83

Power Structures Within Global Networks 84

Politics as Network Behavior 85

Social Classes Within the State 86

Republican 89

Oligarchy 89

Dictatorship 91

Technocracy 91

Transitional 92

Colonies 93

Dependents.. 94

Frameworks for Execution 95

Frameworks for Internal Problems......................... 96

Profitability 96

People Management.. 97

Process Mapping.. 99

Demand Generation 99

Framework for External Problems 100

Epilogue... 103

Introduction

The one quality that sets humankind apart from all other species is imagination. We are not the strongest animals, nor are we fastest. The condition of the average person in modern society—with obesity, drug abuse, and mental health issues running as rampant as they are—points to the fact that we are not the wisest either. Nor are we necessarily the most well-organized; there are clear limits to our ability to work in sustainable peace together collectively with more than a certain number of people.

What has allowed our species to utterly dominate our environment is our capacity to generate fictional ideas, convince other humans to embrace that fiction, and then manifest that fiction into reality. This almost magical ability to both create fiction and transform that fiction into reality is the fundamental key to our ability to adapt to virtually every climate on the planet, to withstand incredible hardship, and to relentlessly pursue goals that seem irrational. The ability to create something material and tangible out of figments of our imagination is the heart of what it means to be a creator.

The true value of an idea, of fiction, is that it multiplies the number of possible available actions to take in any given situation. When they encounter an inhospitable new environment without reliable sources of food, an unimaginative being might either slavishly stick with what worked in the old environment and starve, or try to return to a friendlier place. A being with imagination might convince her fellows that a deity spoke to her in a dream about a new kind of food that they should eat. Or she might be inspired to dig for her more traditional food underground, on the basis of a scientific hypothesis that she has.

Fiction is such a fundamental part of the human experience that we couldn't survive without it—even in the face of a reality that is superior to the fictions we choose to believe. Numerous philosophers across history have bemoaned our reliance on fiction, most famously, Plato. In his seminal work, *Republic*, Plato presents his Allegory of the Cave. In this allegory, prisoners are chained in a cave facing a blank wall. They come to believe that the shadows projected on the blank wall are the real world. They are so attached to this understanding of reality that even if they were dragged out of the cave and could see that their reality was actually just shadows cast by the sun, they would, in Plato's estimation, choose to return to the cave.

More importantly to Plato's point, those who choose to focus on the real source of the shadows in the cave—the sun—would be the first to go blind. Most of us, in fear of that pain and brightness, return to the more pleasant illusions of the cave and choose to live in that fictional reality instead.

We tend to organize ourselves into societies based on shared fictions, or worldviews—defined as sets of complementary ideas that together are used to explain how the world works (ontological) or how it ought to work (moral). These worldviews detail what we believe reality to be and map out the decisions that we prioritize within that fictional reality. Most of us subscribe to one or more worldviews that we ourselves have not created. Building and evangelizing a new worldview is difficult and time consuming. Rather than creating a new worldview, most humans will trade their time and property to pursue one that already exists. This exchange is the basis of the social contract that drives humans to work together. The strength of a social bond is measured by the amount of resources—namely, time and property—that a person is willing to bear to support someone else who shares the same worldview.

Because we are imaginative creatures, our beliefs are malleable. A person can maintain competing worldviews if a single one does not meet their core physical, emotional, or material needs.

The goal of this book is to provide you, the reader, with the tools you'll need to truly become your own person in today's world of clashing worldviews and societal fictions. The starting point for asserting power over your own mind and freeing yourself from someone else's fiction is to create your own—a vision of the world that *you* wish to see. This vision must be a concrete, tangible idea of a future world that is based on observable data from the present. Armed with this vision, you can then create a strategy for manifesting it in reality.

A single voice in a crowd gets lost. A crowd speaking with a single voice is easily understood. No vision of the world can be achieved by a single person, and so for your vision to become a reality, you must share an understanding of your vision with many others. To awaken others to your vision, you must understand them—their motivations, their needs, and their existing worldviews. Strategy is the scaffolding necessary for moving fiction into reality. But when we must work with other people, success relies heavily upon empathy and a keen awareness of the difference between fiction and reality.

This book is structured in three parts. The first part covers how to take control of your own mind and to master the self. The second part covers person-to-person interactions and how to encourage others to embrace your vision. The third part covers how human social networks are structured and how they can be leveraged to help manifest fiction into reality. Each section builds on the principles covered in the preceding section.

Stylistically, this book aims to be concise, but also somewhat open to your own interpretation. It is a handbook, not a textbook, to guide you through the process of becoming your own person and defining purpose for yourself.

The Foundation

BREATH

The first step in the process of transforming your vision of the world into reality is mastering control of your mind and body. This may seem like an odd first step, but it's likely that if you are reading this book, you exist in a state of emotional and physical imbalance.

Our modern world is cerebral. We spend most of our time within our own heads, while simultaneously consuming media designed to validate and magnify our emotional states. Modern technology has not only removed us from nature, but also from the need for physical exertion. The financial demands of life in modern society compel most of us to spend the majority of the daylight hours—and often evenings as well—working at jobs that pay just enough to get us by.

Often, finding a job means moving far away from family and other social support networks. Isolation and loneliness are common, leading to a wide range of unhealthy coping mechanisms. On top of all that, there is the hormonal and biochemical havoc that modern diets wreak on our ability to think clearly.

As we age, we get bent out of shape and become consumed by neuroses we've convinced ourselves are "normal."

What if you could stop all of the noise in your head? The negative self-talk, the guilt, the frustration, the blame, the self-pity, the sadness?

You *can*. The process starts with breathing.

How often do you hold your breath when you are feeling stressed or anxious, or when you're experiencing a strong emotion? How many times do you breathe in the course of 60 seconds when you are feeling relaxed? Happy? Frustrated? What about when you jump into cold water?

Most of us probably couldn't answer these questions off the top of our heads. But spend some time over the next few days checking in on yourself and counting. You might be surprised by how connected your breathing is to your emotional state and your level of energy.

The autonomic functions of your body include things like your heartbeat, breathing and hormone production. They happen without any conscious action on your part. These autonomic functions play a pivotal role in driving your moods and the feelings you experience in response to your interactions with the outside world. There are a few autonomic functions, like blinking and breathing, that our conscious minds can take over when we wish. What's more, breathing is the only physical action under our conscious control that communicates with and affects other autonomic functions. In other words, you can use control over your breath to direct your emotional responses to external situations.

Breath technique is the foundation of every single spiritual tradition based on meditation. It is also central to self-hypnosis and other Western techniques of mind/body control. Even within elite level sports or martial arts, proper breathing technique is seen as essential for maximizing performance and reducing recovery time.

Most of these traditions and techniques focus on deep breathing, which describes breath that originates from the diaphragm. High levels of stress and the resulting physical tension can result in shallow, chest breathing. This acts as a negative feedback loop because chest breathing limits the amount of oxygen transferred to the bloodstream with each breath, triggering a faster heartbeat and snowballing other physical stress responses. Training yourself to instead breathe from the diaphragm will result in noticeable physical and psychological changes. While there are many techniques that you can explore, this simple deep breathing exercise done several times each day will provide the foundation of what you need:

1. First, make sure that you can feel the difference between chest and diaphragm breathing. Place one hand on your chest and one on your stomach. When you take a deep breath in, make sure the hand on your stomach rises higher than the hand on your chest. Repeat until you feel comfortable breathing with your diaphragm.
2. After an exhale, take a deep breath in through your nose, slowly counting to four.
3. Now, exhale through your mouth, slowly counting to eight. Be sure to actively use your abdominal muscles to push all of the air from your lungs
4. Repeat this four times. It is important that you spend twice as much time exhaling as you spend inhaling.

Put energy into making deep breathing your normal breathing pattern, and stay conscious of how you breathe in all situations. Mastering control over your breath is the first essential step to unleashing your full creative potential. The ability to control your breath even when under stress allows you to keep a clear mind. It also helps you more easily enter a flow state, where your energy is focused fully on success rather than in the scrambled thought patterns of panic..

FROM BREATH TO FLOW

Breath control is the key to entering the mental state necessary to effectively manifest your vision into reality.

Without question, we are usually the biggest obstacles to our own success . More specifically, we struggle to separate our self-perception from our learned emotional reactions. Under the guise of "self-acceptance," we train ourselves to identify *as* a culmination of our past actions, thoughts, and feelings. If you naturally respond with anger when teased, then you might see yourself as an angry person. If you tend to flood with contradictory emotions in the face of interpersonal conflict, you might be seen as an "emotional" person. If you come to accept the characterization as an angry or emotional person, you lose the ability to imagine yourself in any other way and come to mindlessly repeat the same thought patterns and behaviors every time you encounter similar circumstances. Over time, the neural pathways for those specific behavioral patterns become so strong that you lose the ability to respond in other ways. Typically, these hardwired neural pathways in your brain will trigger a reaction to a situation without any conscious involvement from your mind. This reaction is a combination of thoughts, emotions, and physiological changes like sweaty palms or rapid breathing. In accepting a fixed view of your emotional and physiological responses, you become an easy target for a devious person to manipulate.

Breath control gives you the ability to create space between yourself and your emotions and thoughts. It allows you to override the hardwired, knee-jerk reactions that your brain has built over time and instead, choose how you wish to respond.

Breath control also gives you the ability to control your perception of time. Time is our most scarce and precious resource; stress and hardwired reactions are thieves focused on stealing it from us. Stress rapidly speeds up your perception of time, generally to the point where you feel that you have less time than you need to accomplish your goals. Hardwired reactions steal your time by constantly exposing you to unintended consequences of your behavior that can distract from or even derail the pursuit of your goals. In both circumstances, you will frequently make inefficient or outright incorrect decisions because you lack space from your hardwired reactions. Preoccupied with your immediate thoughts and emotions, you lose your ability to manage how you experience time.

People who succeed under high levels of external stress—or in creative efforts—often talk about entering what psychologist Mihaly Csikszentmihalyi termed a "flow state," also known as "being in the zone." Csikszentmihalyi developed his theory of flow in the late 1970's while trying to understand the experiences of a number of artist colleagues who reported getting completely lost in their work. Through a series of interviews, he identified six key characteristics of flow:

1. Focus only in the present moment
2. Action without effort
3. Self-consciousness disappears
4. Heightened sense of control
5. Sense of time slowing down
6. Enjoyment of action and the moment

Csikszentmihalyi was not the first to uncover this state. Flow has been a staple of many East Asian and Indian spiritual practices for thousands of years. The use of the word flow itself to describe the state is evocative of the flowing water imagery used in the ancient Chinese Taoist tradition. The seminal Taoist text, *Tao Te Ching*, focuses heavily on the how and why of achieving an active mental state in alignment with the surrounding world. As the *Tao Te Ching* puts it, "action without action." It sounds paradoxical, especially in a world where we associate getting things done with being busy and checking off long to-do lists. By contrast, flow describes the ability to manifest your goals by using the existing energy around you.

The important point is that however you wish to describe it, this state of flow is the end goal of learning how to control your breath to the point that control becomes instinct. The flow state unlocks your ability to understand yourself and the world around you, free of limiting thoughts and unbounded by the pressure of time.

Part 1

The Right Frame of Mind

Once you have mastered the basics of flow, the next step is to cultivate the right mental habits. These are foundational habits that will serve you well in not only creating a realistic, achievable vision, but also in performing the varied cognitive tasks required to bring that vision to life.

MINDSET

There are four mental characteristics that are essential for developing a self-directed mindset:

1. **Commitment** - The most fundamental characteristic. The master demonstrates relentless commitment to and definitive action towards a goal once it has been defined. He executes his plans with the utmost ruthlessness, without hesitation once the decision to act has been made.

2. **Morally Unbiased** - Worldviews, ethics, and social rules can be useful tools to further a strategy. But

you must be free of them when visualizing the future that you want or assessing progress towards your goals. It is impossible to be truly objective—the human brain naturally distorts the sensory information that it receives—but it is possible to remain aware of your own biases in order to avoid falling into crippling cycles of self-judgement.

3. **Curiosity** - Wise people are aware that there is still much to learn, and so remain open to learning. The key to continual self-improvement and mastery is a relentless drive to learn more—more about oneself and more about the world.

4. **Flexibility** - The very nature of a set plan assumes a static world that will predictably and consistently behave how it has in the past. When the world reveals itself to be more dynamic than plans allow, the master has the ability to find and follow an unplanned route to success. Flexibility also applies to attachments to certain beliefs or ways of being.

VISUALIZING THE FUTURE

To be a successful creator, you should be able to envision the future you wish to manifest in ways that are detailed and tangible. One of the best exercises to begin this process is visualization.

Visualization was most notably brought into American popular culture by sports psychologist and mindful meditation teacher George Mumford. Over the past 30 years, he has helped some of the best professional basketball players in the world mentally prepare for competition, including Michael Jordan and Kobe Bryant. Visualization is a type of meditation in which you literally visualize how you will perform an activity in your mind.

Most of the research around visualization has been applied to athletics. It has conclusively found that visualizing an activity activates the same neural pathways as physically performing the activity itself. For example, in a study conducted by Cleveland Clinic exercise physiologist Guang Yue, participants were broken into four groups: one control group, one that did finger and elbow exercises in the gym, one that visualized finger exercises, and one that visualized elbow exercises. Unsurprisingly, the group that actually went to the gym saw an average strength gain of 53%. Also unsurprising was the control group, who saw on average no change in strength. Amazingly, the group visualizing the finger exercises saw a 35% strength increase, while the group visualizing the elbow exercises saw a 13.5% strength increase.

This presents a very clear view of just how much power the mind actually has over the body. Beyond our heartbeats and stress reactions, our thoughts can also affect our muscle memory and our ability to perform physically.

Just like any practice, the benefit of visualization comes down to the amount of effort that you apply. This is not a light, 5-minute daydream about how great it would feel to achieve your end-goal. This is a mental walk-through of exactly how you will go through the process to reach your end-goal. George Mumford has stated numerous times that the most successful athletes he has worked with were extremely detail-oriented in their mental walk-throughs. Sporting champions from boxing, to golf, to gymnastics describe visualizing the entire competition in painstaking detail, from the changing room to the actual venue of play. Down to the details of how they would tie their shoes or where specifically on the court they would take shots during warm-ups.

Developing the muscle memory for actual game situations through visualization has helped athletes like Michael Jordan and Kobe Bryant get into flow states when the time came to perform in real-life. In a way, everything they did on the basketball court had already happened in their minds hundreds of times before. These mental repetitions allowed them to "act without action"—without having to worry about what they would do in any given situation—so that they could fully immerse themselves in the moment.

We can apply the lessons gathered from how athletes use visualization to other areas of life as well. Whether you wish to create a business, a political movement, or simply improve some aspect of yourself, the process is the same. You can use visualization to do a mental walk-through of the specific actions that you will take to accomplish your goal.

The goal may change over time, but the visualization in your mind must be concrete and tangible. The purpose of visualization is not to create a fantasy view of the world, but rather to create an explicit, tangible view of the future derived from an understanding of the observable world.

Forcing yourself to visualize your goal in detail is also a good way to see whether it is tangible enough to be worthy of pursuit or whether it still needs to be developed more thoroughly. Abstract terms and isms are not vision. Concepts like "liberty" and "freedom" are not real things. Descriptions of states of being are meaningless if they can't be touched or directly experienced through the senses.

Begin by closing your eyes and imagining the world exactly as you wish it to be. Imagine, in fine detail, the experience of waking up in the morning. What is your first interaction of the day? What is your morning routine? What were the specific steps that you took to bring this world about? Who did you work with to get to this point? What does your personal office look like - do you have pictures of loved ones on your desk? Does your office not have any desk at all, and maybe instead is outdoors? And so on.

The more detailed your vision, the better conditioned your mind and body will be for recognizing opportunities for success *and* acting on them without hesitation. Practice visualization regularly.

DESCRIBING THE FUTURE IN A TANGIBLE WAY

Visualization will help prime your mind and body to pursue the actual future you want deep down. The next step is to put that tangible definition of what your desired future actually is in writing. This process is the very first literal step in bringing your ethereal vision into physical reality, and it also serves as a basis for communicating this future to others who might work with you or share your goal in a relatable way.

You must first define your end goal in terms that are specific, measurable, action-oriented, realistic, and time-based. SMART.

S = Specific	Compare the strategy of "Help women get high-paying jobs" with "Help female college graduates get engineering jobs at technology companies in Silicon Valley." The more specific your goals are, the more precise your planning will become.
M = Measurable	You need to have the ability to measure success from either a qualitative or quantitative standpoint, preferably both. Compare the strategy of "Grow the economy" with "Increase Gross Domestic Product by 3%."
A = Action-oriented	A tangible goal must demand a specific course of action, and should not simply be a statement of support for a worldview. Compare "I think that rape is a terrible thing" with "I will develop education programs that reduce instances of rape on college campuses."

R = Realistic	Can you accomplish this goal with the resources at your disposal? There is no point in working towards goals that have no reasonable prospect of success. Compare the goal of "Convince the United Nations to stop all global warming by 2025" with "Convince my local Congresswoman to vote "yes" on the current CO_2 emissions reduction bill being debated right now in Congress"
T = Time-based	A strategy should have a definite end-point to help ensure that execution is happening at the appropriate level of intensity and pace. Compare "Increase the number of trucks being produced by 200%" with Increase the number of trucks being produced by 200% within the next 2 years"

The Time-based part of the visualization process is often overlooked. However, it is important to respect the fact that the universe is not orderly and that over time, things that are currently stable become unstable. By putting clear time boundaries around your end-goals, you put yourself in a position to keep your goals in line with changes that are happening around you in near real-time.

GOALS VS. STRATEGY VS. TACTICS

Up to this point, we have spoken about goals and visions of the future. Those two concepts can be seen as one and the same thing. A vision is a snapshot—how you want the world to be at a specific moment in time in the future. Goals are the elements of that vision on which you can focus energy to make into a reality. To actually make your goals in reality, you will need to develop strategies. And after that, tactics for executing these strategies.

Although the terms are used interchangeably, strategy and tactics refer to very different things.

Tactics are the tools and means by which a discrete, static milestone or goal is accomplished. Their use is situational, and depends not only on the goals at hand, but also on the specific environment within which you are operating. Strategy, on the other hand, is a high-level roadmap for achieving multiple goals over a long period of time. It is the sum of vision, SMART goals, and organization supporting execution. Most importantly, it is a fluid and constantly changing target.

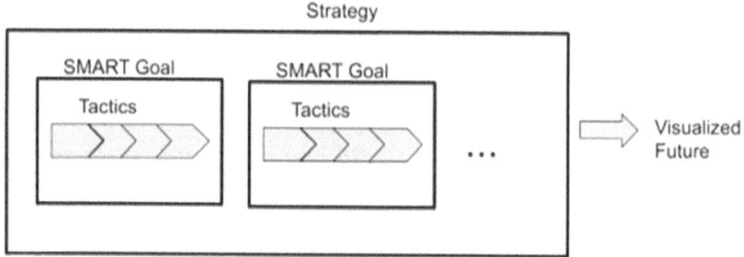

In real life, there are people who are great at getting the first 10k customers, winning the election, or raising that first round of capital. And then there are people who know what to do when they get there.

The tactician only thinks about how to reach the next milestone, and as a result, constantly tries to defer the consequences of past choices. The strategist sees the current milestone, as well as the next 10, and is prepared for all of the loose ends that eventually turn up.

The tactician runs in sprints, and so their accomplishments may look spectacular to the untrained eye. The strategist is running a marathon, and so their accomplishments are only spectacular in retrospect, when their plans are fulfilled.

IMPLEMENTING TACTICS

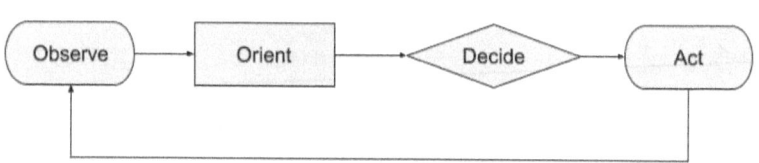

OODA is a useful heuristic for continually adjusting your tactics in real-time. It was initially developed by United States Air Force Colonel John Boyd for application by fighter pilots, but is a relevant framework for tactical responsiveness across many contexts. Instead of creating a Plan B to your Plan A—which only encourages a lack of commitment to Plan A—OODA can be used to skillfully pivot in order to stay on course for achieving Plan A. While all components are necessary, the Observe component is the foundation of all good decisions. Superior orientation and decision-making skills cannot, over time, compensate for an inability to completely and objectively assess what exists in the surrounding world.

OODA stands for:

O = Observe - appraising the actors and their interactions within a given environment, in as unbiased a manner as possible. Measure how your previous actions have affected the overall environment.

O = Orient - analyzing what has been observed through the lenses of past education, past experience, and instinct.

D = Decide - determine the best course of action to take. This is the best opportunity to develop a hypothesis or assumption to test.

A = Act - execute selected course of action.

In particular, OODA provides a means of measuring one's own execution with that of any opposition. In a conflict situation where your vision competes with those of one or more other people, tactics should include those that disrupt the "Orient" component of the opposition's OODA loop. The ability to control the opponent's perception of the environment can help overcome deficits in resources and expertise.

By successfully controlling the opponent's perception of the world around them, you can disrupt their ability to orient themselves properly. In this way, your own goals become increasingly opaque while theirs become more transparent.

While most obvious in real-time situations, OODA loops can be applied to much longer time-scales, and are useful even as a tool for evolving a strategy as the environment and surrounding actors change. Instead of diverting energy towards a Plan B, you can use OODA to help make necessary changes to Plan A. However, the primary benefit of OODA is that it provides an opportunity to learn from mistakes.

Learning only through tactical or strategic failures will often leave you without enough time, resources, or support to recover. Better to stumble and quickly catch yourself than to fall flat on your face. The value of a model such as OODA is that it allows you to make and correct errors of judgement as you execute your tactical plan in real-time. It forces constant observation and adjustment, which may seem tedious or obsessive. However, when you are in a flow state, your mind naturally runs through OODA smoothly and rapidly. When you watch an athlete in the zone, you will see that they still make mistakes. However, the quickness through which they cycle from a mistake to corrective action prevents their opponent from gaining any advantage.

FAILURE

Failure is the inability to accomplish a SMART goal or to fully execute a strategy. It is the result of a persistent inability to learn from tactical mistakes or to correct bad individual decisions.

Tactical failures may be recovered from and corrected if you are fortunate enough to have the available time and space. However, strategic failures are often fatal unless you are able to make numerous, *correct* structural changes to your approach in order to correct your course. Do not rely on learning from failure as your primary means of getting your strategy right.

SUCCESS

Success is the point at which the SMART goal or strategy has been achieved, and thus is binary. Either you have succeeded, or you have not. There are no degrees of success. Falling short is failure, while likewise, far exceeding your goal is not meaningfully different than just barely succeeding. And if you consistently blow your goals out of the water, *you have been setting the wrong goals*.

If you fail to accomplish your SMART goals, then your strategy will fail. If your strategy fails, then your vision will not be realized. This may sound harsh, but understand that in our current-day high stakes war of worldviews, you should not expect 2nd and 3rd or more chances at accomplishing your strategy. If you truly want to be self-directed, you *will* make others feel threatened enough to attack you—socially, verbally, financially, or even physically. You must build a flexible strategy without contingencies, focused only on success. You cannot live in a house that you have half built, and you cannot win a race if you run only half the distance.

"Win or learn" may sound success-oriented, but at its core, it assumes continued participation even after failure, and all of the space and time necessary to implement the things you've learned from failure. Investing in Plan B in a high stakes environment signals a lack of definitive action and commitment to building a successful strategy from the start.

Bet all-in on Plan A, and make success your obsession. Force yourself to mentally commit to your plans once you make them, and you will find opportunities to aid success where you least expect them. If you don't fully commit, you will instead find excuses for failure.

MYTH OF THE ORDERLY UNIVERSE

A wise strategist will recognize that she is just as subject to her own ego as the people she seeks to influence in her pursuit of her strategy. The worst of the traps laid by her ego is the belief in the possibility of an orderly universe. Chaos and entropy are normal states of the universe. The strategist's belief in an orderly universe is built around her anxieties of not being in control. The fiction of ultimate control is an immediate cue for action and provides a short-term sense of purpose. But the impossibility of realizing that fiction creates horrifying cognitive dissonance and crippling anxiety in the long run. There are no perfect strategies, perfect plans, or perfect tactics. Only successful ones.

The belief in an orderly universe—either a moral or literal order—can drive inaction in key moments as the strategist seeks the perfect plan. It can snatch defeat from the jaws of victory, as the strategist seeks not just success but glory, and the mantle of "greatest ever." It can drive mental breakdown in the face of disastrous failure.

Often, the most expedient tactics for pursuing a strategic milestone may conflict with one's sense of how things "should be done." Take a good look at the world today—at who has the greatest influence over the aspects of the world that you wish to change. How many of them play by the same social or ethical rules of how things "should be done" or how people "ought to act"? There is an extremely strong correlation between people who create their own rules and the ability to bring substantive change to some aspect of the world. Now think of the influencers who developed the rules that you follow. How many of them were deemed to be unethical, illegal, or immoral?

Rules, social mores, and ethical systems are meant to provide momentary stability in a universe where chaos and disorder are constant. They are created to address very specific current or foreseen problems. Applying them inflexibly will severely limit your ability to generate strategy and the tactics necessary for executing your strategy.

Therefore, before developing any kind of strategy, you must be relentless in questioning the original intent and current usefulness of the social or ethical rules that you personally follow. More importantly, you must determine whether upholding those values is more important than living in the kind of world you wish to see.

ENDS VS. MEANS

There has been much discussion across history about whether the ends justify the means. The morally unbiased strategist understands that whatever means they employ must not create cognitive dissonance or confusion among those who are crucial to the execution of her strategy. No other criteria matter.

CONTEXT AND ZEITGEIST

In addition to having SMART milestones, a strategy must be aware of the dominant worldviews and ideas within the target environment—referred to as the zeitgeist. Zeitgeist is what makes the vision behind each strategy meaningful, rather than arbitrary. A strategy such as "Increase the number of female software engineers in Silicon Valley by 10% in 5 years" is only meaningful because the zeitgeist indicates that there aren't enough female software engineers in Silicon Valley.

Zeitgeist shifts based on both exogenous (external) and endogenous (internal) effects. Exogenous effects include an influx of new people or materials into the environment, or shifts in climate that affect human behavior. Endogenous effects include shifts in power dynamics between genders, ethnic groups, generations, or other small subgroups of shared special interests. Both can change unpredictably, which makes it necessary to treat strategies as evolving, adaptable targets that are continually tested and improved, rather than as static, unchanging declarations uttered in corporate-speak.

The unpredictable nature of the zeitgeist also necessitates an organized effort to monitor the various networks within your environment and their composite members. Also important is the way that information cascades within those networks, and the way that their members engage with the outside world. By gathering thorough intelligence in this way, you can learn to anticipate changes in the zeitgeist and, in time, precipitate them.

LUCK

Understand that your vision of the world will not come about by chance. For each thing that you passionately wish to see in the world, there is someone who likely detests it with an equal amount of passion. The master does not rely on luck for success. If you attempt to create strategy without a clear vision or without SMART goals, then you are relying on luck. If you expect multiple opportunities to try and fail and try again, then you are relying on luck.

There is a difference between being lucky and being prepared to exploit a sudden opportunity. Being lucky involves success by pure accident. Being opportunistic involves a keen awareness of your environment, rapid pattern recognition and moving through an OODA loop at speed to get a step closer to your goal.

PROBABILITY

The master strategist does not make fear-based decisions. Most people have a tendency to give more weight to decisions that avoid bad outcomes rather than those that pursue rewards. In fact, humans are generally biased towards loss avoidance. Daniel Kahneman, who won the 2002 Nobel Prize in Economics, along with mathematical psychologist Amos Tversky, developed Prospect Theory in the late 1970's in an attempt to explain this phenomenon. They noted that the way a person frames an outcome in their mind affects their expected benefit. In other words, if someone stands to lose a lot—even if the probability of loss is low—they will perceive a lower benefit from the potential reward, even if the reward is large. They called this "Narrow Framing."

Given that the subconscious mind is susceptible to suggestion from the conscious mind, making calculations based on the probability of failure rather than success keeps you oriented towards opportunities for failure rather than opportunities for success. Good strategy evaluates only the probability of success and does not focus on the expected loss or probability of failure.

The easiest way to avoid Narrow Framing and escape the loss avoidance trap is to hone the "Realistic" aspect of your SMART goals. A strategy built around SMART goals that have a high probability of success will help reduce the psychological pressure that comes with a fear of loss. Instead of flooding your mind with anxious thoughts, you can fully focus on simply executing actions that you have already visualized yourself doing.

Decision trees are a simple, commonly used tool for comparing the expected outcome in the event of success versus failure. They are a valuable tool for overcoming the Narrow Framing problem that happens when a proposed action is only judged through a subjective lens. The basic model for calculating the benefits of each branch of the decision tree is as follows:

If I succeed: $V = P \times O$

If I fail: $V = (1 - P) \times O$

Where probability (P) refers to the likelihood (expressed in percentages) of the event happening, and expected outcome (O) refers to the magnitude of reward or loss, expected value (V) refers to the product of probability and expected outcome. You can use this formula to compare the expected value of multiple options as a simple way of quantifying the option with the highest expected value.

This same approach can be used to evaluate different options that involve sequences of follow-up decisions that must be made, as follows:

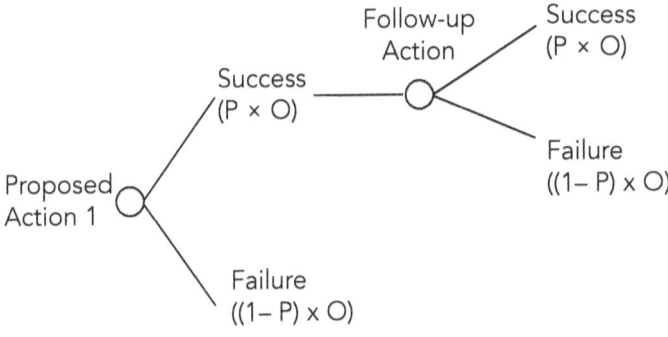

FIRST HAND VS. SECOND HAND INFORMATION

Because bias affects how we perceive information, we must take great care to describe things that are observed firsthand in as uncolored and objective terms possible. We may be tempted to apply certain heuristics that separate "important" from "unimportant" in order to speed up decision-making, but we mustn't skip steps within an OODA loop. It is better to make a single good decision deliberately than to make multiple poor decisions. Thus, be sure to be mindful and non-judgmental when gathering first-hand observations about your environment.

When operating in complex or very large environments, it may be necessary to rely on second-hand information about the observable environment gathered from other people. For these observations, an even greater level of care should be taken. Do not allow feelings towards the source—positive or negative—affect the level of effort that you make to assess the reliability of the information that you receive. Additionally, you should be well aware of your source's biases in order to gain a clear sense of how the information you are receiving might be colored. Consistently unreliable sources should be filtered and assessed to determine any overt or subversive worldviews that they may intentionally be attempting to push in opposition to your own.

Of the two, first-hand observations are much more reliable—even when the second-hand source is an "expert." This is not to be dismissive of those with subject matter expertise. Instead it's meant to highlight the fact that even experts can struggle to make good decisions. A great example is the medical field, where patients regularly have to deal with medical experts who misdiagnose problems due to overlooking crucial behavioral data points when investigating symptoms or being dismissive of information shared by their patients.

The secret to the talent of making unbiased observations of the surrounding world lies not in knowledge of the world, but rather in awareness of one's own biases.

PRINCIPLES FOR TAKING ACTION

There are two primary principles to consider when taking action:

1. Move with urgency (moving rapidly through OODA is the best way to correct bad habits or lacking discipline early—moving hesitantly through OODA to avoid making missteps limits your ability to learn).

2. Maintain your ability to move through OODA without skipping steps (if you move faster than your ability to respond to changes, you've lost your ability to observe and re-orient based on outcomes from your earlier actions).

RESEARCH AND AVOIDING SURPRISE

The leader who thinks she knows it all or believes that the universe can be controlled is highly vulnerable to being taken by surprise. Surprise is the state in which a person finds themselves after encountering a reality previously understood to be entirely impossible. While a person cannot plan for all possibilities, it is possible to avoid being surprised by getting a thorough sense of what you know and staying open to amending that list. You must embrace the reality that the universe is chaotic and that what you know to be true could be completely wrong. The only thing that you can control is how you respond.

Awareness of the blind spots in your own knowledge is essential preparation for the unexpected. Extensive and unending research is the only way to continually ensure speed and accuracy in your ability to Observe and to Orient. It is also the only way to maintain a strong sense of timing—the ability to anticipate the beginnings and early direction of a shift within a shared environment faster than your opposition can.

A person who is ready will respond to the unexpected with intent, and so is able to adapt even when under duress. A person who is unready will react to the unexpected out of instinct, and will only succeed due to sheer luck.

Part 2

Working with others

The focus of the previous section was the process of applying the principle of flow to the process of developing tangible goals towards your vision and executing upon those goals. But even if your goal is simply self-improvement, there will come a point where you need to enlist support from others. To recruit well, you will need to get out of your own head and see the world from the perspective of those around you in order to persuasively communicate your goals. You will need to understand and navigate the worldviews that frame how those around you engage with the world.

It is important to remember that the vast majority of people that you encounter also suffer from the same types of physical and psychological stress that you do. Their behaviors are likely to be driven more by hardwired, knee-jerk reactions than by measured, thoughtful responses. And they probably don't consider your understanding of the world to be self-evident.

It's easy to fall into the trap of thinking yourself smarter than everyone else because you have insights that most lack, or to get frustrated about how people don't respond the way they "ought to" to your brilliant vision of how the world should be. If you are struggling to persuade others of the value of your point of view, **it is your fault, not theirs**. It is not their job to care about your vision—they have their own myriad of issues they are struggling through. It's your job to persuade them that your vision can help them with their issues more so than any other worldview that they currently hold. All of us are entrenched in our current worldviews and patterns of behavior. To make changes, people need a compelling "What's In It For Me?"

In order to do that, you must apply the elements of flow to your interactions with others—specifically, the principle of separation from self-consciousness. In order to better understand how to demonstrate the benefits of realizing your vision to others, you will need to hone your ability to see the world solely through other people's perspectives.

Broadly, there are two ways of getting people to work with you: having them trust you, and coercion through either threat of violence or extortion. Only the former is self-sustaining. Those who gain cooperation purely through coercion are, over time, forced to spend valuable resources on the necessary steps to follow through with threats. Otherwise, those whom they have compelled will walk away as soon as the perceived ability to follow-through is low enough.

Trust, on the other hand, requires nothing more than occasional validation of the belief you have fostered that there *is* a "what's in it for me?" in cooperation. So here, we will examine the barriers to building trust and how to overcome them.

BIAS - THE DECISION-MAKING TOOLKIT

Classical economic models and political theories treat human beings as optimizers of rational outcomes. They assume that we either have perfect information or that we rationally engage all of the information that is available in order to make decisions. However, as the fields of economics and political science started to focus on the psychology behind decisions, a new and more nuanced understanding of human decision-making has emerged. One in which our decisions can be best understood not by what we know or what our goals are, but rather by the biases we use to process information.

Bias has a very undeserved reputation as something problematic that must be eliminated. However, that ignores the important role that bias has played in the iterative development of the human brain over the last

2 million years. What we call biases are merely reflections of how the software that is the human brain operates. And they allow us to create decision-making models much more adaptive and responsive to environmental change than all other mammals. Our technological accomplishments and ability to not just survive but thrive in virtually any of Earth's many climates are consequences of our ability to use biases to navigate within a chaotic universe.

From an objective view of modern society, many of our biases lead to irrational behaviors. For example, political pundits on TV often discuss the concept of people voting against their own interests—where voters fail to see the disconnect between the attractive rhetoric of politicians they vote for and the actual policies of those politicians once in office. In another example, one can often observe highway drivers in a hurry weaving through traffic and as a result, taking longer to reach their destinations. In both cases we see bias preventing people from proper pattern recognition in the heat of the moment, and as a result making irrational decisions with sub-optimal outcomes.

However, our evolution as homo sapiens has never been a process of becoming *more* rational. It is instead a process of successful iterative adaptation to changes in the environment over long periods of time, with a healthy dose of randomness. An OODA loop, of sorts, that plays out thousands of times over each generation. From a biological point of view, biases have served an important role in helping humans to not only adapt better than virtually all other mammals, but also to develop advantages that have grown into planetary supremacy—for better or for worse.

The major biases that shape our decision-making are:

Anchor bias—giving undue weight to the very first piece of information received

Availability bias—overestimating the importance or reliability of information that is most readily available

Appeal to authority—giving undue weight to an argument based on the academic or social credentials of the person making the argument

Bandwagon bias—adopting a belief simply because other people have that same belief

Blind-spot bias—the ability to see how the biases held by others impact their judgement but failing to see the same in oneself

Choice-supportive bias—rationalizing a poorly constructed decision

Clustering illusion—finding patterns in events that are actually just random

Common sense bias—the belief that something must be incorrect because it contradicts what one believes to be intuitively true

Confirmation bias—seeking out or accepting only information that confirms our existing beliefs

Conservatism bias—favoring prior evidence over new evidence regardless of the strength of new evidence

Information bias—tendency to seek additional information, even when it does not add value towards making a decision

Ostrich effect—ignoring information that is negative or threatens the ego

Outcome bias—judging a decision based on its outcome and not on the information available

Overconfidence bias—overestimation of one's abilities

Placebo bias—an experience caused solely by the belief that the experience will happen

Recency bias—favoring newer information over older information

Salience bias—focusing on the most easily recognizable features of a thing or idea

Selection bias—expectations influencing perception more heavily than actual observable data

Sunk cost bias—favoring a previous, costly decision over a new alternative to avoid taking a loss

Survivorship bias—judging an experience based only on information from those who succeeded and ignoring information from those who failed

Zero-risk bias—evaluating options through the lens of what is lost in the event of failure

EGO AND THE INDIVIDUAL

Like virtually all living systems, the human body aims to remain inert. It constantly wages war against the powerful forces of death and disorder. It requires an immensely strong sense of self, manifested in what we call the ego, to keep our fragile bodies alive. The ego is the combined set of psychological responses to both the outside world and our physiology that drive behaviors of self-preservation. These responses serve to alter the objective world as we perceive it into subjective worlds that match our respective senses of self and align with our worldviews.

The end state of self-preservation sought by the ego is an inert state of physical and psychological comfort. So, the ego's response to an endogenous (internal) factor, like the feeling of depression, might be to drink until the discomfort of depression is numbed. The ego's response to an exogenous (external) factor like blazing summer heat might be to crank up the air conditioner and lower the temperature until the body feels cooled down.

Economist and Nobel Prize winner Herbert Simon identified a mental model that most of us go through to determine a state of comfort that we deem acceptable, which he called Satisficing. Satisficing is a decision-making model that a person uses to choose a minimally acceptable option where information about the best possible choices is limited or non-existent. We are subject to many biases that narrowly frame our perceived courses of action and there are also things we know we don't know. At the same time, most of us pursue courses of action that provide a short-term comfort payoff. As a result, instead of the "best possible" decision, we tend to look for the first option that meets our standard of what is acceptable.

As a result of the Satisficing model of chasing comfort, the more comfort that a person feels their current situation can provide, the more difficult it is to create a change in their behavior—even if the proposed change would result in even greater levels of comfort.

UTILITY MONSTERS

On March 12th, 1930, Mohandas Gandhi began his famous 240-mile Salt March to the Indian coastal village of Dandi in protest of British salt taxation laws. His original group of 79 swelled to over 50,000 by the time he reached Dandi on April 6th. News of his protest spread throughout India, and inspired millions more Indians across the country to mount their own protest against the British Raj's salt tax laws by making their own salt.

Twenty-five years later, in Montgomery, Alabama, a group of Black community leaders led by Jo Ann Robinson and Dr. Martin Luther King Jr. organized a bus boycott in response to Rosa Parks' famous arrest for refusing to obey racial segregation laws on a city bus. What started out as a one-day protest—during which 90% of Montgomery's Black citizens refused to ride the bus—became a 13-month economic boycott of the city's bus system.

These events are not exceptional because of their scale, or even because of the significant political change that they facilitated. History is full of governments that have collapsed under threat of mass revolt by hungry peasants or coups instigated by widespread dissent within their militaries. It is not so special to revolt when there is nothing to lose. What is supremely rare is for people to make a sustained sacrifice of things that they currently consume—especially for something as essential as transportation or easily accessible salt—in order to achieve a bigger goal.

This kind of sacrifice represents a highly unusual dedication to a cause that required most participants to give up the small level of comfort they had to fight entrenched structures seemingly far more powerful than themselves. In general, people commit to their values up to the point that those values conflict with their ability to maintain their status quo. When it comes to making sacrifices, most of us will sacrifice our stated values rather than our ability to consume. We are, after all, loss-averse creatures more than we are reward-seeking.

The dominant political philosophy of today's world is liberal democracy. The ideas of 18th and 19th century Enlightenment Era thinkers are so deeply ingrained all over the world that even governments with no intention of actually practicing liberal democracy feel compelled to use its language. Single party dictatorships and parliamentary democracies alike call themselves Republic or Democratic in an effort to appeal to the "power to the people" political zeitgeist of our modern era.

One of the core concepts behind liberal democracy in practice is an idea popularized by 19th century English political philosopher John Stuart Mill—Utilitarianism. At its core, Utilitarianism is a political calculus that evaluates a public policy option based on the number of people who benefit from it against the number of people for whom it causes suffering. It weighs the perception of all people equally. In theory, a policy is considered to be worth pursuing if it results in more people benefiting than suffering.

However, even in countries that could objectively be considered liberal democracies, we see very non-utilitarian policies getting passed that effectively transfer wealth from a majority to a very small minority. Why is that?

The real issue, as philosopher Robert Nozick pointed out in his 1974 critique of Utilitarianism, is that most of us are Utility Monsters. Most classical economic and political models—Utilitarianism included—treat governments and their composite citizens as uber-rational beings constantly seeking an optimally harmonious arrangement of society. Utilitarianism weighs the perception of all people equally. This generally works in small groups, where everyone regularly sees all other members of the group. However, in very large societies, most of us tend to weigh our own pleasure more than the suffering of people who we do not see or interact with at all. Our own pleasure is tangible, while the suffering of an unknown stranger is not. We become what Nozick calls Utility Monsters—beings who gain a greater amount of perceived benefit from the sacrifices of others than the total amount of suffering *actually* caused by said sacrifices.

The lesson here is that humans are not naturally inclined to give up current privileges or benefits to stop the suffering of others to whom we are not directly connected. In fact, we are prepared to ignore a great deal of *even our own* suffering if we perceive our personal benefit from that suffering meets our Satisficing standard.

THE ROLE OF WORLDVIEWS IN SHAPING BEHAVIOR

As human beings, we organize our lives in pursuit of psychological and material comfort. However, the process of visualizing the futures that we want, and then developing goals to achieve those futures is difficult. And we are each born into a society that is already moving at full speed, with socioeconomic hierarchies that tell us our place and how to view the world. Our lives are guided by worldviews, or shared visions of how the world ought to work.

Worldviews guide not only our understanding of how the world ought to work, but also, of how it works right now. While the individuals who hold a worldview may not see it, each worldview contains SMART goals and is part of someone's or some entity's strategy for world domination. It may seem humorous to think of rural political beliefs one day influencing decision-makers who have global reach. But remember, the early Christian church was viewed as a tiny breakaway sect of Judaism in 64AD, when Roman Emperor Nero blamed it for the Great Fire of Rome. Nearly 2000 years later, Christianity has become one of the preeminent spiritual and political worldviews on the planet. The lesson is that worldviews will either spread or die. And it should be no surprise that many who try to spread a worldview have self-interested ulterior motives.

Take liberal democracy as an example. Although we have little control over the worldviews that we are born into or grow up with, we do have a choice about what to believe once we reach an age of self-awareness. Abandoning the dominant worldview of where you live does not come without consequences. Due to our pathological pursuit of comfort, we are especially reluctant to sacrifice current Satisficing comfort for a future of social marginalization. We work hard to convince ourselves that there is no other better way of life than our liberal democracy and its economic system, in spite of clear data that the average person has unresolved mental health issues, exercises poor diet, gets poor quality sleep, is increasingly poor, is increasingly obese, and our environment cannot sustain how our economy demands that we live.

We defend that worldview because we're deeply invested in it. We've signed away 30 years of income to a bank in return for a house on a ¼-acre plot of land that we can say we own. We've signed up for tens of thousands of dollars of non-dischargeable debt in order to get a certificate that says we're employable. We've thrown thousands of hours away watching our favorite actors and TV programs. Since the dawn of the Internet Age, gratification has gotten closer and closer to truly being instant. And our desire for instant gratification, justified by the "pursuit of happiness" mantra of liberal democracy, has created unimaginable wealth for stakeholders within the industries that prop up the entire system. For those who have embraced the Utility Monster mindset, spreading the worldview of liberal democracy is a means for expanding their own wealth at the rest of the world's expense. Continued participation by voters and consumers who themselves feel invested via their participation provides a moral legitimacy to the whole process.

In a sense, the choice to accept a worldview is a transaction with the expectation of material or social benefits. Material benefits generally involve increased or guaranteed levels of consumption, and therefore personal comfort. Social returns revolve around external validation or gains in social status. Acceptance is defined here as the extent to which behaviors are consciously tailored around conformity to dominant worldviews.

COGNITIVE DISSONANCE

We adopt worldviews across various aspects of life. We may employ one worldview to direct how we engage with people at our jobs and another to direct how we manage our family lives. There are no neat boundaries between these contexts. Very often, these worldviews will conflict. The psychological stress caused by holding two conflicting views is called cognitive dissonance. Because we are creatures who flee from stress towards comfort, the typical response to cognitive dissonance is either mental gymnastics, or a weakening of both beliefs.

Mental gymnastics is a form of choice-supportive bias. It is an attempt to out-logic the contradiction created by simultaneously held that conflict and re-create a narrative in which both worldviews can exist. It is an exercise in futility, but a normal response by someone deeply invested in both worldviews. A Sunk Cost Bias will lead them to "double down" on mental gymnastics until the trigger of the conflict is gone. Someone engaged in mental gymnastics is extremely closed to revising their worldview, and will continue well beyond the point of absurdity.

The common response by someone only weakly invested in one or both of the worldviews is a weakening of their acceptance in one or both. In the immediacy of the discomfort of cognitive dissonance, they are most open to revising the worldviews that they accept or even adopting replacements that meet their Satisficing threshold.

THE UNCONSCIOUS MIND

We saw from the breathing and visualization exercises that in a relaxed state, the mind is very receptive to suggestion. We can influence unconscious, autonomic functions in our bodies through breath. We can build real muscle memory by doing a detailed run-through of an activity within our minds.

Through suggestions directed at the unconscious part of the mind, we can influence future thought patterns, including openness to new ideas or even worldviews. The literal definition of the unconscious mind is the content of one's memories, worldviews, and biases, of which our conscious minds are unaware in the present moment. For example, a person may unconsciously choose to use a plastic bag rather than paper for their groceries when given a choice. In the moment, their conscious mind heard the request "Paper or plastic?" and delivered the response "Plastic." But they did not consciously make the decision. Instead, within their unconscious mind, a consumerist worldview and regular memory of giving the same response to the same question hundreds of times before came together and generated the decision.

Unlike the ego, the unconscious part of your mind does not have a preferred state of being and does not judge what it experiences. It merely stores information and performs information processing tasks that the ego gives it.

In a flow state, the unconscious mind is running the show. Your body is taking instructions directly from the unconscious. Because the conscious mind is shut down, your unconscious is not constantly being interrupted by the usual stream of judgements and random thoughts. Visualization is an exercise where the conscious mind trains the unconscious mind how to respond when in a flow state. Video is such a powerful medium precisely because it replicates this practice closely. People who watch TV shows for hours on end find themselves in a stupor that superficially resembles flow state. The clear difference between flow state and the TV-induced stupor is that your whole being is engaged when in flow, while mindless TV shows only engage your unconscious.

Lacking the captive attention that video commands, many retail stores and casinos attempt other tricks to communicate directly with our subconscious minds. They rely on sensory cues to trigger memories of specific emotions that increase the likelihood of certain behaviors. In retail environments, things like enjoyable music, bright colors, enticing smells, or even maze-like layouts may encourage a shopper to buy more. Casinos often go for sensory overload, with an excess of flashing lights, machine noises, attractive wait staff, and even free alcohol to disorient the conscious mind but drive an urge to play the slots or blackjack. In both cases, they bypass the conscious mind when marketing themselves to customers.

Influencing the unconscious mind is a major part of influencing others. If you are proposing a vision for a different worldview or even just a change in daily habits, you will need to overcome the Satisficing "good enough" of the current comfortable status quo. The most effective way to overcome this is not by convincing the conscious mind, but by changing how the unconscious mind frames the choice.

MECHANICS OF INFLUENCE

There are broadly two ways to influence others' behavior:

Direct Triggers—direct, explicit calls-to-action

Indirect Triggers—emotional cues or unconscious suggestion

Direct Triggers refer to influence that is explicitly exercised. They appear in relationships defined by a strict hierarchy that is acknowledged by both those who give the commands and those who receive the commands. Authority only flows downward from those in dominant positions, while obedience is expected of those in subordinate positions. Generally, these are only useful for influencing specific behaviors within existing worldviews.

Indirect Triggers refer to influence that is exercised in a non-obvious or an unconscious manner. They appear in relationships where either hierarchy is less clear, all actors occupy the same level within a hierarchy, or a subordinate within a hierarchy has a greater level of influence. Influence is driven not by authority, but by triggering predictable emotional reactions. With indirect command, authority may travel upwards within a hierarchy, known as "pull."

INDIRECT TRIGGERS

Most cultures that claim democratic values have an official policy of equality, and most places in the world will at least put on the pretense of being democratic. What this means in practice is that Direct Triggers are only used in specific contexts where you have unquestioned authority to issue commands. Unless you are a very senior level person in the workforce or a parent, a majority of your interactions will be with relative peers. Use of Direct Triggers with people who do not look to you as the source of authority will be met either with resistance, or the optics of bullying.

Indirect Triggers focus on presenting your audience with ideas that spark a specific emotional reaction or implant a suggestion within their unconscious minds. These triggers can occur in one of two directions: push or pull. In the classic "carrot or stick" contrast in motivational styles, push techniques are the stick (force/punishment), while pull techniques are the carrot (bribe/reward).

PULL TECHNIQUES

Pull techniques involve connecting with desires for either present or future reward. These are typically things that your audience feels are lacking in their lives and that their conscious thoughts have suggested their unconscious minds to pursue. Some examples include:

Social acceptance—motivates those who experience social exclusion that negatively impacts quality of life.

Sex—motivates those who are fixated on sexual satisfaction, sexually frustrated, or eager to prove their virility.

Wealth—motivates those who are fixated on wealth accumulation and those who have anxiety about money.

Food—motivates those who use food as a source of psychological comfort or who have food insecurity.

Social status—motivates those with lower social status, those insecure in their social position among their immediate peers, or those who fear authority.

PUSH TECHNIQUES

Push techniques involve connecting with fears and anxieties that have been internalized by the conscious mind into biases. Some examples include:

Loss of Social or Gender Role—Used to generate anger, desire for violent response. Often presented in a factual way, with heavy name dropping to demonstrate credibility. Often presented as an appeal to self-defense or defense of a broader social group.

Immorality—motivates those who see themselves as enlightened. Used to generate outrage or force social exclusion of the immoral subject. Often presented as a core trait, with single actions used to define the subject's entire nature. If the subject is popular with the audience, behaviors or traits are highlighted that create a strong sense of values dissonance for the audience. Even if claims are shown to be objectively false by a third party, the sense of dissonance remains in memory. A common example is false claims about an opponent in political attack ads during a campaign for election to public office. Attack ads aren't meant to present the truth, but rather create moral doubt on the part of undecided and lightly committed voters.

Loss of physical choice—Used to generate a wide range of emotions, including fear, anger, distress, and demoralization. Can be a reference to non-consensual sexual contact, physical confinement, invasion of personal space, threat of violence, or involuntary limitation of normal daily activity choices. Can also be loss of assets, ability to consume assets, or access to assets. Driven by a sense of loss of human dignity, self-respect from feelings of embarrassment, shame, violation. The key is a fear of material loss that will also lead to greater loss of freedom of action.

Loss of life—motivates all. Used to generate terror and willing concession of physical choice in return for removal of immediate perceived physical danger.

Loss of culture or identity—Used to generate outrage, anger, desire for social exclusionary or violent response. Can refer to social status, way of living, or sense of importance. Relies on existence of hierarchical social structures, clearly defined gender or social roles, and regular rituals.

DEBATE

The only useful purpose of debate is to understand how deeply someone holds one or more worldviews, and how they respond to cognitive dissonance. You will rarely state your position so eloquently or forcefully that you will change another person's mind. Instead, use debate as a form of research into how they perceive the world and how they process information.

If you debate well, your debate partner will tell you indirectly how to change their mind. If you are debating someone to score points or to "win," you are merely engaging in narcissism. Which is a waste of time.

SWAYING THE MARGINALIZED

A person who accepts the prevailing worldviews of their community sees themselves as doing what is good or what is right. Questioning their behaviors that conform to those worldviews will most likely be met with resistance. The key to unlocking that resistance is identifying the points at which the individual's fundamental self-perception is higher than the role assigned to them within the worldviews they follow. An example of this would be a family-friendly startup that highlights its company culture to lure a working mother away from her job at a competitor dominated by young, childless employees.

SWAYING THE ZEALOTS

For zealots or for those who enjoy privileged social status within the current set of worldviews, worldview dissonance is not an effective tactic for gaining influence. Resistance and mental gymnastics will likely be prohibitively strong. The best approach for influencing these individuals is by appropriating worldviews and out-zealoting the zealot. Because you are dealing with individuals who are highly invested in the current set of worldviews, you will need to offer a costly signal as proof that you have an even greater level of investment/privilege. It need not be a real investment—merely one that satisfies the perception of realness to those who themselves are highly invested. The more privileged the individuals that are you are dealing with, the more social proof you will need to back your costly signal.

 A good example of the appropriation technique is the use of an ultra-conservative blog that disseminates fake news appealing to a nationalist mindset but is subliminally prompting specific voting decisions that have nothing to do with nationalism. The approach was used to great effect on social media channels like Facebook by the Russian intelligence apparatus to influence the 2016 Brexit and America presidential election outcomes. Here, the costly signal is the supposed effort in maintaining a website and sourcing the news articles. The approach works by presenting information that aligns with the worldview and unconscious motivations of the subject. In this way it avoids any cause for resistance to influence.

MANAGING UNCERTAINTY

We are pattern recognizing machines. We default to focusing on familiar patterns; but our perception of these patterns is shaped by our egos and by the worldviews to which we are exposed. We relentlessly pursue the fictional worlds—full of comfort and happiness—promised by ideas that are shared with us. We pursue them to the extent of giving up time and resources to achieve their promise.

When uncertain about how to decide or act, when the ideas we believe in fail to produce the comforts our egos desire, we revert to magical thinking. Magical thinking works by reducing the complexity of the problem at hand, making it more "understandable" in order to help make a judgement. Unlike popular belief, it is not a symptom of a lack of education, but rather of prolonged cognitive dissonance between the ego's understanding of the world and the reality that is experienced. It is a product of the anxiety that arises from cognitive dissonance between how one's ego perceives the world and one's actual reality. The anxiety may be the barrier to making a clear-minded decision, or the dissonance itself may be enough to make the person feel completely disoriented.

Magical thinking sees the world through simple, generally binary narratives like good vs. evil and us vs. them. Because magical thinking is a product of a sense of powerlessness, it leads to reliance on an outside force that gives simple, unambiguous guidance on what to do—guidance that the person feels safe obeying without having to think about "why."

It is a mistake to think that only a certain type of person is susceptible to magical thinking. All of us have at least one area of our lives in which we are unable to properly orient ourselves to make decisions that lead to success, and so revert to magical thinking.

Part 3

Group Level

Mastery of interpersonal, one-on-one persuasion is absolutely critical to getting others to embrace your vision. However, materializing your vision requires more than just a one-off conversion of non-believers. It requires the ability to build networks and leverage those networks to execute your SMART goals.

Managing networks itself is an artform. In some ways, networks act as a macrocosm for individual decision-making. But in other very important ways, networks have their own behavior patterns that are distinct from how we behave as individuals. Very often, the whole is much more (or if poorly led, much less) than the sum of its parts.

FOUNDATIONS OF A NETWORK

At its core, a network is a collection of individuals. There are different levels at which we operate—at an individual level, at a family level, at a community level, and then, at a global level. At each level, there is a core need around which people will organize themselves and adopt worldviews to fulfill.

At the individual level, the core need is **personal comfort**. We can understand personal comfort as a state free of internal and external stress. All of the activities that a person engages in, both consciously and unconsciously, are biased towards preserving that sense of comfort.

At the family level, the core need is **support**. A nuclear family unit is generally the smallest level at which multiple humans will organize themselves, while extended families and clans willingly join in a network only to the extent that they can expect near-unconditional mutual support—be it emotional, financial, or material. Note that family level networks are generally households, roommates in shared living situations, work/sports teams, support groups (such as Alcoholics Anonymous), educational cohorts, friend groups, and social clubs. Leadership may or may not be formal and roles in general may be nebulous and interchangeable.

At the community level, the core need is **wealth**. A community can only be said to exist when individuals and families join in a common network for the specific purpose of enabling its members to share, sustain, or generate wealth. Wealth can be tangible—like money or commodities—or intangible—like a shared passion or set of psychologically nourishing values. Community level networks are things like businesses, schools, non-profit/NGOs, religious groups, trade associations, homeowners associations and community organizations. They generally have budgets, own assets, and employ at least part-time staff. Leadership structure is formal, but lower-level roles may be less well-defined and even high-level leaders might wear many hats.

At the global level, the core need is **singularity**. At this level each node within the network sees itself as an extension of the whole. Rejection of incongruent elements is typically firm and decisive because the driving urge is for oneness and harmonious alignment among members of the network. Note that global level networks are generally managed by actual governments or other formal bodies that have the power of policing and taxation. Leadership is highly structured, hierarchies of power are often rigid, and there is a wide range of specialized lower-level roles.

There are generally two conditions in which individuals and groups of individuals may decide to move up one level and establish strong bonds.

1. The core needs of their current level are clearly met. So, for example, an individual who feels secure in possession of shelter, warmth, and other markers of personal comfort may decide to get married, have children, and start a family.

2. The core needs of their current level are unmet, and the individual makes the calculus that they would be if the individual invested in a higher level of network organization. So, for example, a community that is struggling to protect its wealth may decide to invest in membership in a global network in order to secure its own long-term wealth.

THE HUMAN MACHINE

Social groups or organizations function similarly to individuals in that their net behavior is shaped by internal and external factors, and that there is a group-level ego (worldviews) geared at preserving the cohesion of the group.

While the core principles of influence remain the same as at the individual level, the ability to manage human networks is key to scaling influence beyond just one-off interactions.

Influencing groups of people can be important to strategy—both as a means of organizing resources to execute decisions, and as a part of an end-goal.

DEGREES OF SEPARATION

Within a human network, the idea of degrees of separation refers to how directly or indirectly one human is connected to another. Having one degree of separation, or being a first-degree connection, means that two people are directly connected to one another. Two degrees, or a second-degree connection, means that two people who are not directly connected to one another are both directly connected to a third person. Three degrees means that two people each have first degree connections who themselves are first degree connections. And so on.

Many have sought to identify the maximum number of degrees between any two randomly selected humans on Earth. American playwright John Guare popularized six degrees as that maximum number, while various research attempts at finding this number using social media or email networks have been inconclusive. The exact number is not important. What the research has demonstrated is if information takes more than five or six degrees to reach every single member of a network, there are severe issues regarding the interconnectedness—and by extension, the overall sustainability—of the network.

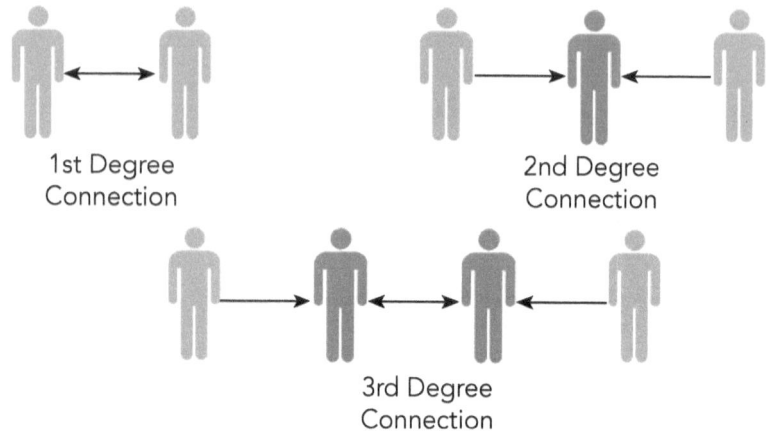

TACTICAL RESOURCES

When executing on decisions, there are two primary types of resources: the human resource and the non-human resource. Human resources refer to the methods for engaging people or groups of people to take part in decision execution. Broadly, these methods can be grouped into "indirect" and "direct" command.

Non-human resources refer to the systems, channels, and assets mobilized by human resources, and include things like financial, physical, and information assets

COMMUNICATING PUSH

The channels of communication techniques are best determined by the resources available, the information consumption habits of your targeted subjects, and the existing influencers who your subjects currently follow.

Where information is ubiquitous and noisy, one-on-one communication can be ineffective at large scale. Delivering the same repeated message from multiple sources that the subjects within a network, community, or social group are normally exposed to help ingrain the message in their memories above all of the other noise.

Managing Networks or Organizations

NETWORK COMPOSITION

Human networks are made up of people who share information and resources based on the strength of relationships they have with others within the network.

It's important, when managing networks, to be aware of how relationships are distributed. Research by British anthropologist Robin Dunbar suggests that there is an upper limit to the total number of strong and weak first-degree connections that an individual can sustainably maintain. These are bonds of friendship, family, and acquaintance through shared activities. They generally develop organically.

Because they are primarily composed of people who are all directly connected to each other, most family and community-level networks operate within this threshold. The worldviews shared within these networks are generally informal—a byproduct of the organic nature of the bonds that keep the network together.

Networks large enough that most individuals are separated by two or more degrees will naturally decay over time. Formal rules that are regularly reinforced through ritual and formal structures are necessary to keep the network and its underlying worldviews intact.

Ideologies that believe in global adoption of a worldview without these structures in place to hold that global network together are practicing Magical Thinking.

WEAK VERSUS STRONG BONDS

Within the language of networks, each member of the network is called a node and each node is connected to at least one other node via social bond. The bond between nodes is based on a shared social contract that is based on the worldviews that frame the broad behaviors of the social group. This social contract promises future material reward and privileges in the present in return for investment of time and resources to support the goals espoused by the worldview.

The average person in this information age is exposed to many competing worldviews. Being bombarded with so many different social myths and ideals weakens one's attachment (and therefore investment) to any single one. The dominant worldviews held therefore become less of a conscious choice, and more baked into our subconscious.

The first worldviews that most of us hold are an accident of birth, a product of decisions made across multiple generations. If we enjoy a privileged status or can expect relatively high future rewards, we are likely to keep those worldviews at our core, even if we adopt different worldviews as we age. In general, the strength of a bond is defined by a combination of the frequency of interactions between the two parties and the length of time over which these interactions have occurred.

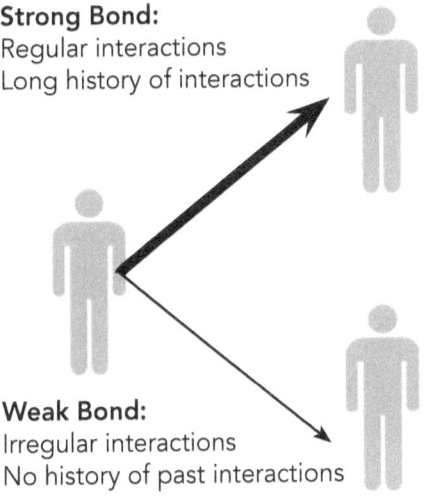

Strong Bond:
Regular interactions
Long history of interactions

Weak Bond:
Irregular interactions
No history of past interactions

Humans are generally subject to the sunk cost bias—we give undue weight to past investments when making decisions about the future. We can exploit this bias to determine the strength of a person's bond to a particular social group. A strong bond will drive a person to make significant sacrifices in time or resources to support someone else within that social group, based on the sunk cost of past investments made in the group. A weak bond is characterized by either only verbal support or support that stops once personal comfort is affected.

A common mistake that organization leaders often make is to demand that new and less privileged members make sacrifices on behalf of the group before they have enjoyed benefits of membership. If these new members have not made substantial investment to join the network or if they have not yet had time to develop strong bonds within the network, such demands will alienate rather than inspire loyalty.

STRUCTURE

If organizational styles were measured on a continuum, one end of the continuum would be spider style while the other would be starfish style. The spider style relies on top-down leadership, where all decision-making is hierarchical and generally only flows downwards from leaders to followers. On the other end of the spectrum, the starfish style relies on all members of the group having the ability to spread and execute the core message as necessary, such that there is not a single center of control driving organizational behavior.

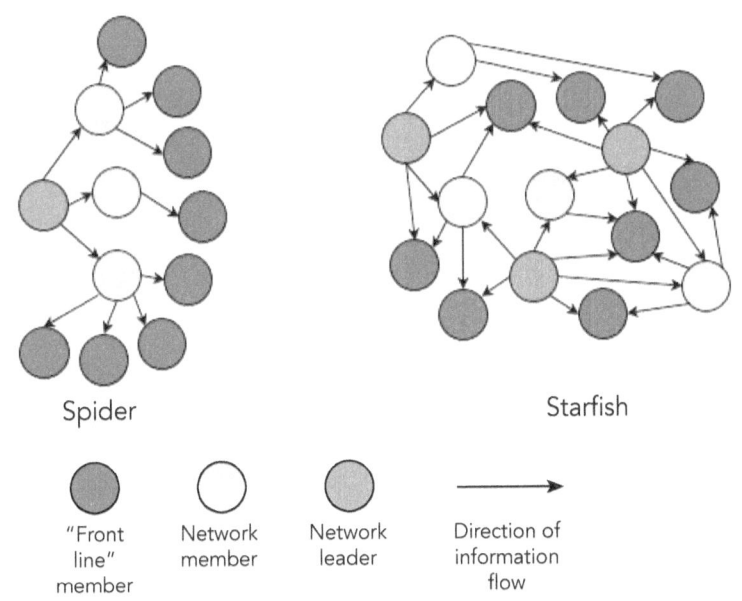

COST OF INFORMATION SHARING

Information degrades as it is shared across multiple nodes within a human network. A clear message between two first degree contacts will be less clear between two points in a network separated by four degrees. We live in a world in which information is currency. Our brains deconstruct information as it is received, and then convert it back into information oriented towards our individual egos and biases. Information is then used to make decisions about things, and shapes the information we in turn share with other nodes within our networks.

There are three parts to the conversion process—time spent finding or receiving the information (R), time spent deconstructing the information into data (D), and time spent creating a shareable interpretation of that data (I). Finding the information involves all of the time and energy spent simply acquiring data—either intentionally seeking it or receiving data transmitted to us (for the latter, compare the time it takes to read a short message with the time it takes to watch a 2-hour tutorial video). Deconstructing information into data is the **Observe** process within an OODA loop—identifying the tangible, measurable elements of the information received. Finally, creating a shareable interpretation of the data is a combination of crafting an internal understanding of the data and deciding how to convey that understanding to others.

It's important to recognize and be aware of proportionally how much time is typically spent in each phase. OODA loops at the organizational level need to account for:

1. Information that contains ground-level data from front-line "implementers" cascading up to decision-makers in order to start the Observe process.

2. Messages from decision-makers cascading down to front-line "implementers" in order to jump start the Act process.
3. Consistency of information as it passes through various nodes, who each apply their own individual biases as they reconstruct information they receive for further sharing.

Organizations with a high velocity of information (V) typically find themselves able to act faster than competitors. So long as information exchange between nodes is fairly lossless, high velocity organizations can maintain a competitive advantage even if facing a resource disadvantage. Overall, the golden ratio is V = (D + I) / R. The higher the value of V (velocity), the faster network members are turning information around to the decision-makers who rely on them.

Therefore, when leveraging a network for influence, there are several points of consideration:

1. degrees of separation between originating nodes (decision-makers) and terminal nodes (front-line implementers).
2. the time it takes to propagate information between two nodes within the network.
3. the time it takes for the originating node to observe the decisions made by the terminal nodes.

4. whether or not there is a need to obscure the identity of originator nodes.
5. the types of biases that affect how various nodes interpret and share information.

Therefore, the optimal structure for leveraging or influencing human networks is highly dependent on the scale and frequency of information that needs to be cascaded across the network.

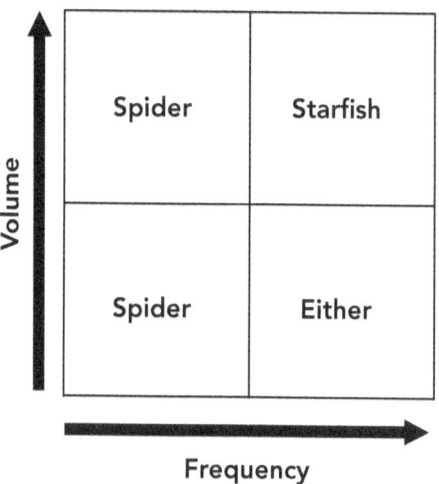

DIVERSITY OF PERSPECTIVE

While part of the cost of information sharing can be greatly mitigated by the structure of the network, the part of cost related to the warping of information with bias as it cascades across network nodes is more difficult to manage.

The warping of information comes down to intent. Intentional warping happens when nodes within the network willfully attempt to subvert decisions made at the organizational level or to sabotage other specific network members. Warping is generally due to low personal investment in the network's mission and/or culture, where the offending node is not sufficiently invested in the social contract of the network.

Networks with high levels of cultural diversity will struggle with both intentional and unintentional information warping. High levels of cultural diversity will invariably result in some nodes who harbor historical resentments against the network due to having stronger bonds with other victimized networks. This will encourage willful subversiveness and perhaps even an unconscious desire to destroy the network. Also likely to warp information are nodes who are marginalized within the network due to deliberate assignment of lower privilege by the prevailing network worldviews.

At the same time, diversity in life experience can be a useful asset in decision-making, as it allows for higher levels of creativity in team-based problem solving. It also helps to ensure a more thorough process of observing the outside world, which is the foundation for making consistently successful decisions. To avoid subversion or the problems in weak bonding, it is important to recruit diverse nodes into the network and aggressively reward their good-faith participation. Strong bonds will ensure that these nodes Orient the data that they receive from other nodes in accordance with the network's worldview, and ensure lossless communication of information.

TRUST AND VIOLENCE

The foundation of any social contract, economy, or human network is a single entity or coalition holding a monopoly on lawful violence. Participants "consent" to this monopoly in order to ensure that the rules of the network are enforced. There is no other sustainable method of maintaining peace within diverse networks of competing interests. This is true regardless of the predominant worldview—be it democratic, totalitarian, capitalist, or any other organizing ideology.

Potential counter-examples of communes, sharing, or barter-based economies only highlight this reality. How does a participant within such an economy enforce agreements with other participants? Within small groups, where all participants know each other personally and more crucially, are highly aligned in behavioral norms, social pressure alone can prevent or limit bad faith participation. However, as the network grows, and interactions occur between people who do not know each other or between people who hold differing sets of behavioral norms, formal rules and formal enforcement of rules become essential for guaranteeing good faith participation.

Networks that rely only on high levels of trust and honor systems are *particularly* vulnerable to being destroyed or subverted by bad faith participation. They are generally networks that choose to delegate total responsibility for violent enforcement of norms to outside peer networks or to a larger, higher order network. One example is that of households delegating enforcement of personal property rights to a municipal government. Another is that of businesses delegating enforcement of permitted business practices to licensing bodies.

High-trust networks can often encourage bad faith participation when they exceed a certain size because there is low risk and high reward for doing so. While bad faith is unavoidable—there are many who are dishonest by nature—its effect can be managed. Rules-based and trustless networks have greater stability for large diverse networks because they offer incentives for good faith, disincentives for bad faith, and punitive force for repeat offenders. They increase the risk and lower the reward for bad faith behaviors.

Rules-based networks rely on a trusted central authority to create and enforce the conventions that govern interactions within the network. Trustless networks—blockchains, for example—are a subset of rules-based networks. While most rules-based networks are governed by network members, trustless networks delegate this central authority to a rules-based protocol that defines the conditions that must be met for two or more network nodes to interact.

As we have seen with fiat currencies, rules-based networks that rely on trust in humans acting as central authority are very prone to bad-faith actors gaining control over levers of power and abusing that trust. We are at the brink of a revolution towards financial systems governed by trustless conventions because these systems do not require network participants to share worldviews with each other or close bonds with specific nodes acting as central authority in order to transact.

Nonetheless, even actors within trustless networks are subject to centralized, rules-based systems. People attempting to launder money via blockchain-based cryptocurrency, for example, still run the risk of running afoul of local, centralized law enforcement. The last resort of formal enforcement of rules is the punitive use of violence against bad actors. Without the ability to use force in rules enforcement, bad actors can and will undermine the integrity of the network by abusing the trust of those who participate in good faith.

Of course, violence is always a double-edged sword. Sufficiently powerful bad faith actors can subvert or destroy the network if they can challenge its leadership's monopoly on violence. Bad faith actors proliferate where rules enforcers are unable or unwilling to back up the threat of violence with definitive action. This is ultimately how many rules-based networks experience hostile takeovers by bad faith actors who are more willing to use violence than those with legitimate authority to do so.

NETWORK MAINTENANCE

Networks or social groups are not static. In environments with a high volume of competing worldviews, there is a high opportunity cost to investing in any particular social contract. At the same time, as fortunes change, the return on investment offered by a social contract will change. The privileges associated with a strong bond to a network will invariably rise and fall in value relative to those in other groups. As a result, a rational strategy by many who have low levels of investment in the social contracts most available to them is to maintain multiple weak bonds, waiting for the benefits of a strong bond with one to increase enough to significantly outweigh the opportunity cost of forgoing other options.

To keep a network of strong bonds intact, periodic revisions to the social contract must be made to either increase the perceived value of future reward or current privileges of network membership. Care should be made to ensure that the network has leverage to make future changes whenever necessary. There is a point of diminishing returns in increasing privilege or attempting to boost the value of membership rewards.

For key individuals within a network, separate accommodations should be made, in addition to the standard social contract. These are individuals who possess rare, specialized skills, unique natural talents, or access to resources essential for the network. The determination of "key" comes down to the cost of replacing the value that a given individual brings to the network. If the cost of replacement is higher than the cost of a separate arrangement (and the threshold of "higher" is unique to the needs of the organization), then a separate accommodation is worthwhile.

Power Structures Within Global Networks

A global network is a supernetwork made up of many highly interconnected individual networks with many members who have strong ties to members of other networks.

POLITICS AS NETWORK BEHAVIOR

In spite of the passions tied to political positions and how much emotional weight the average person might put on a single highly contentious policy issue, the general strategic direction of a global network is largely shaped by collaboration (and often collusion) between key players across multiple networks.

With this collaboration and the rigid power structures inherent to networks large enough for diverse member value systems comes information asymmetry.

Information asymmetry refers to differences between network members in how much of the total information available within the network is known. It can be a product of differences in general exposure to information as well as warping of information by bad faith actors.

And with information asymmetry, disinformation may be leveraged to prevent existing networks from reshaping or new networks from forming, with the goal of entrenching the social or resource advantages of those sowing the disinformation.

In general, global networks evolve high-level governing structures to provide a relatively clear boundary around the networks that share some form of social contract or agreement to share a geographic or even virtual space. This governing structure—which can be loosely labelled as "state"—serves as the central platform around which smaller networks emerge, and the point of reference for various role types, social groupings, or economic classes that emerge.

These roles will differ based on the core social and economic activities of that network. Historically, these networks were either state-based, trade-based, or religion-based. However, the rise of the corporate structure and the proliferation of purposes for which corporations have been used has created a much bigger range of use cases.

SOCIAL CLASSES WITHIN THE STATE

An individual's ability to jump from one class to another will vary based on the dominant worldviews of the network—specifically, their openness to conferring higher status with increased investment.

The purpose of the state is to administer and enforce—with violence at times—the rules of the global network. The leaders of the network—either in terms of development of worldviews or control of the resources consumed by the network—are broadly the Entrepreneurs, the Rent Seekers, and the Creatives.

The majority of the network are **Workers**—those who trade agency and labor for the benefits of participating in the network—and the **Dependents**—those who have no agency to trade and are complete subjects of whoever chooses to take responsibility for them.

Entrepreneurs are the very small fraction of network members who create the structures within the network that encapsulate worldviews and distribute their benefits to network members. In spite of the typical association of entrepreneurs with business, an entrepreneur may be a politician, business owner, or indeed *any* profession.

Rent Seekers are those who own and desire to extract value from the assets and capital used by the network. While some entrepreneurs may also desire to do these things, the primary difference is that rent seekers don't actually try to create social structures or networks. Rather, they attempt to take over whatever structures already exist.

Creatives are the management and skilled specialist class—they provide process management and subject matter expertise within the structures created by Value Creators.

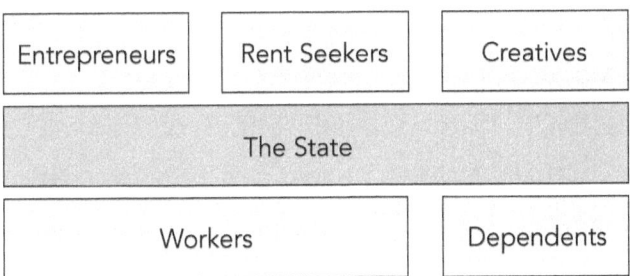

Power dynamics are defined by the relationships that exist between the Entrepreneurs, Rent Seekers, and Creatives. While the activities of Workers and Dependents can episodically impact those dynamics, members of those two groups are constrained by a lack of the necessary agency to conduct organized activity as a group over a sustained period of time.

Additionally, the boundaries between groups can vary or change in fluidity. In systems with high distribution of power, lower-level networks like individuals, families, and communities can change status and move from one group to another, or even occupy multiple groups simultaneously.

Throughout world history, we have seen each group develop the desire to seize control of the state global network. This has been through control over the military or police, control over formal law-making bodies, and control over capital. The nature of the state government will be a reflection of both the specific relationships between individuals in the network, and of broad relationships across these dominant social groups. There are five general natures of a global network—"republican," "oligarchic," "dictatorial," "technocratic," and "transitional." While the general archetypes are laid out here, in reality, stable global networks will often present themselves as hybrids of two or more archetypes.

REPUBLICAN

The republican network structure is defined by a higher degree of social mobility that is made possible by Rent Seekers generally accepting high levels of social mobility for Creatives and Workers in return for a greater level of influence over the State. Relationships between Rent Seekers and Entrepreneurs are still present, but are broadly more competitive than collaborative.

A key ingredient for this formation is a relative balance of power between the Entrepreneurs, Rent Seekers, Creatives, and Workers. The openness to social mobility and high distribution of power is made possible by sustained high levels of economic growth. Another key ingredient is that all groups trust the state as a neutral and relatively honest referee of the network's worldviews.

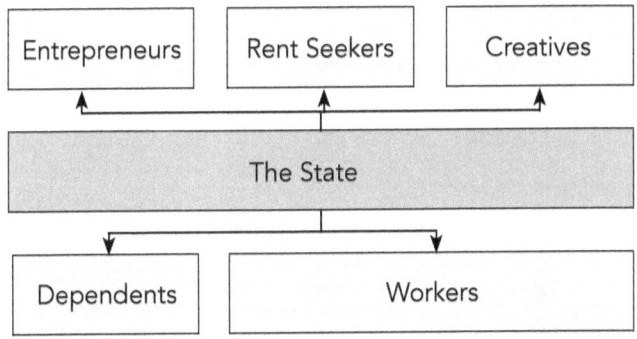

OLIGARCHY

An oligarchic network is marked by significant collusion between Rent Seekers and Entrepreneurs oriented towards capture of the state. Oligarchy may express itself in a feudal form—where Rent Seekers are the dominant class. It may also present an authoritarian form—where a small cabal within the Entrepreneur group has captured a majority of state power and appropriated agency from the Rent Seekers. In both cases, control over the state gives control over Creatives and Workers.

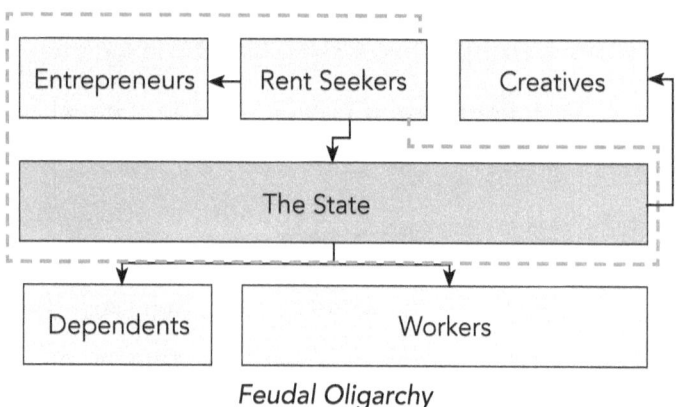

Feudal Oligarchy

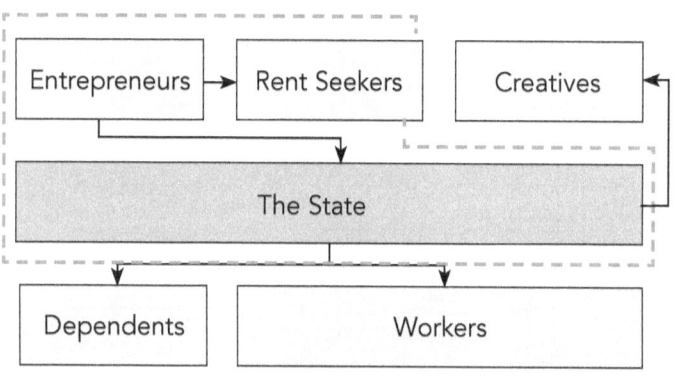

Authoritarian Oligarchy

DICTATORSHIP

In a dictatorial network, a single Entrepreneur or tightly organized cabal of Entrepreneurs has captured a majority of the state's power, leveraging tight direct control over the Creative and Worker classes in order to outflank the Rent Seekers' control over resources. Like in oligarchy, social mobility will likely be discouraged via strict service-based social hierarchies in order to maintain loyalty towards the cabal of Entrepreneurs.

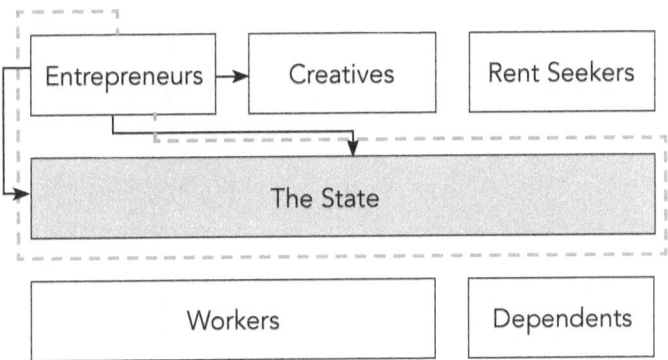

TECHNOCRACY

A state network is technocratic when power largely resides in the hands of bureaucrats and skilled technicians such as lawyers, doctors, and academics. Policy-making is largely delegated to committees of subject matter experts and decisions are largely made via process-driven consensus. Labor and firm activity is largely directed by state-run central planning bodies.

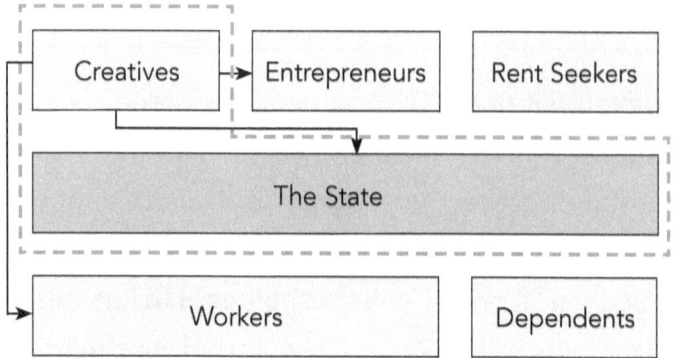

TRANSITIONAL

A state network can be said to be in power transition when Rent Seekers or Workers have captured the state and seek to control it on their own by marginalizing Creatives and Entrepreneurs. This system is called transitional due to the high degree of instability it typically brings. Transitional power arrangements generally come into place following the complete breakdown of a state and its social contract. They are characterized by control over official state institutions, but relatively weak control over other classes. A high degree of internal violence is typical, as is direct competition between community and even family-level networks. The formation of new networks is most common in this phase. As they solidify and consolidate power, transition makes way for one or more other network type.

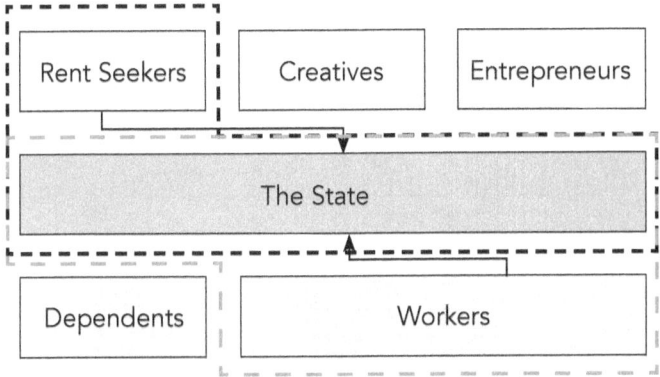

COLONIES

A state network that has been captured or colonized by another state network may take this transitional appearance as well, when the parent-child relationship between the state networks is largely extractive on the part of the parent state. In the event of colonization, a quasi-transitional state is viable so long as the child network itself maintains *some* form of non-transitional network type.

The Rent Seekers from the parent network would therefore maintain financial or political control over the ruling class of the child network. Typically, the Rent Seekers in this network type also maintain strong ties and influence within the parent state to protect their status within the child state network. Often, the parent state sees them as essential tools in maintaining long term control over the child state—particularly in the modern era, where hard colonial power and direct occupation of foreign states via the military is widely frowned upon.

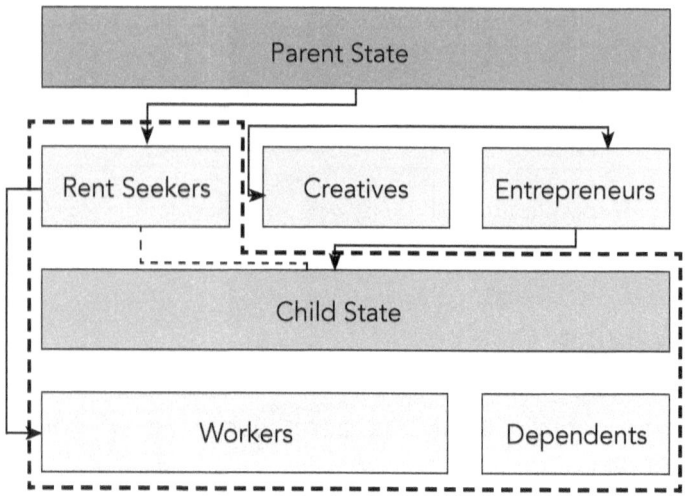

DEPENDENTS

Dependents are low-agency "freeriders" within the state global network. The most common and numerous Dependents are children, followed by the elderly who require support for basic day-to-day functioning. Dependents can also include working age adults who are physically or mentally unable to participate as Workers. Their participation in the network is largely at the whim of the groups who control the state.

In state networks with greater balance of power, Dependents are typically afforded social protections from overt exploitation. In less balanced state networks, their treatment may range from total marginalization and neglect to active enslavement.

Frameworks for Execution

The final component of group-level coordination is ongoing execution. While identifying and driving an initial strategy is itself hard work, there is truth to the old adage of "everybody has a plan until they get punched in the mouth." Neither the world nor your competition is static. Even as you craft your vision and lay your plans, your job as a creator involves making continuous adjustments to ensure that you stay on course as unexpected issues arise.

Fortunately, most of the issues that you will encounter can be broken down to fit within common patterns. Frameworks are mutually exclusive and completely exhaustive approaches to these common patterns that allow you to very quickly identify root causes and potential solutions.

As your network evolves in size and scope, the pressures to which you will need to respond will change. In the short term, taking an intuitive approach may work to solve one-off challenges. But as a general practice, using frameworks to quickly find the root causes of problems will allow you as a leader to increase the speed at which you move through OODA loops. Ultimately, you should be able to respond to changing conditions faster than your competition.

Note that frameworks are tools that need to be adapted to your own individual skills and competencies. The following sections outline common frameworks that should serve as a starting point for developing your own. You should feel comfortable combining, adjusting, and even adding your own elements as necessary. These are not meant to be rigidly applied or memorized.

FRAMEWORKS FOR INTERNAL PROBLEMS

The simplest way to break down possible frameworks is according to whether the organizational challenge is an internal or external one. Internal challenges refer to suboptimal outcomes that are a product of some kind of dysfunction within the organization. There are broadly four internal areas in which frameworks can be applied: Profitability, People Management, Process Mapping, and Demand Generation.

PROFITABILITY

The most commonly used framework within business is the Profitability Model, often used when assessing the factors behind disappointing profit figures. By building out an exhaustive issue tree, it becomes much easier to direct information gathering to ultimately find the core factors that negatively impact profitability.

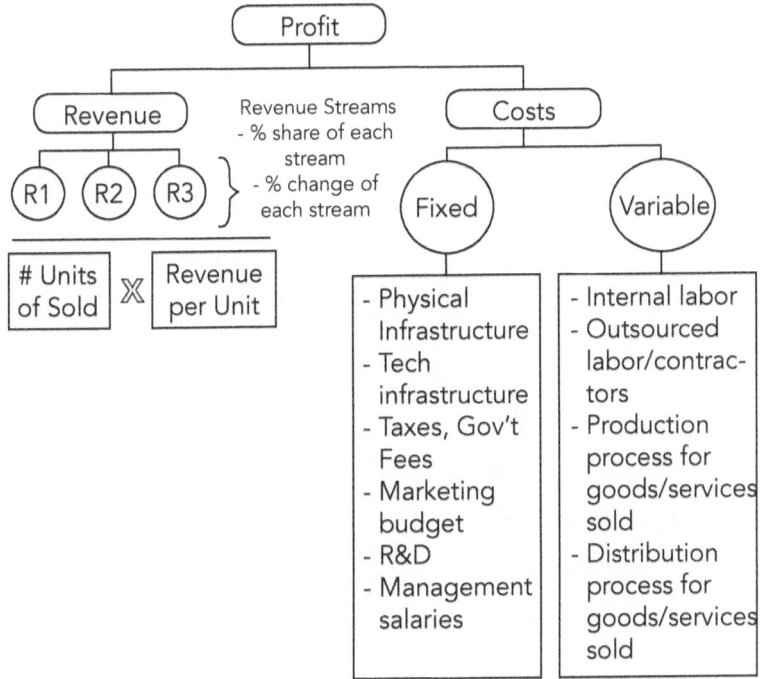

PEOPLE MANAGEMENT

The primary goal of People Management frameworks is to identify the competencies present and lacking within your organization. A common reason why so many creators fail is that they take a "warm bodies" approach to staffing key roles within their organizations. Or worse, they discount the value of intangible skill sets related to relationship building, operational efficiency, and the ability to acquire new skills.

Reframing the Ulrich and ASTD Competency HR Models creates a radar chart covering all functions required by your organization. The Ulrich model was first introduced by "father of modern HR," Dave Ulrich, in 1995 as a framework for reimagining Human Resources as more aligned with corporate strategy. The ASTD Competency model was originally designed by the Association for Talent Development as a rubric for trainers of business professionals to navigate career growth.

In this retooled version, competency areas are split into four mutually exclusive, completely exhaustive groups. Across these groups are three concentric circles, each representing an increased level of mastery. Placing key members of your organization on the chart by function and level of mastery provides a clear view of not only the maximum level of competence you can expect, but also areas where improvements are necessary.

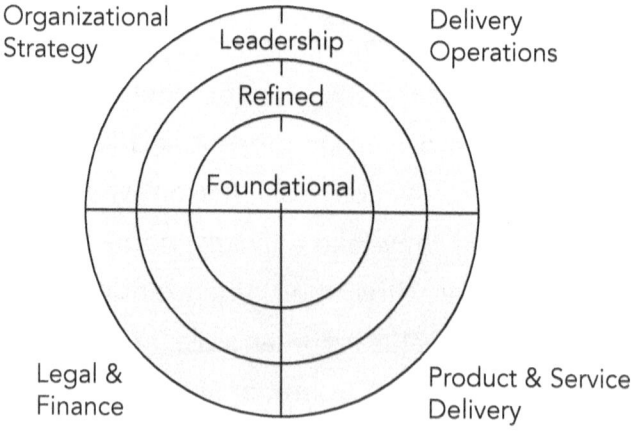

PROCESS MAPPING

A step-by-step process map is a simple way to quickly diagnose the source of problems within a production or operational process. At its core, process mapping involves abstracting the process in focus into discrete, individual, chronological steps, with arrows indicating the direction of workflow movement. Adding the people involved and actions taken within each step allows this to be combined with a people management framework to determine if points of failure are the result of having the wrong people or the wrong processes.

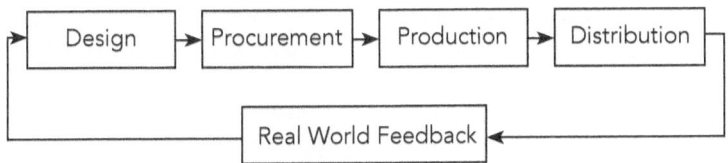

DEMAND GENERATION

Growth-oriented organizations are especially concerned with questions about demand generation. The sales funnel is the most widely used framework for surfacing issues that undermine customer, user, or network member acquisition. The shape is based on the general principle of acquisition, where an unknown segment of a general audience is actually willing to take a desired action. Each section of the funnel represents a set of activities designed to identify that unknown, "willing actor" segment.

The sales funnel model is a strong framework for maximizing the percent of that willing audience who actually takes the desired action, and for discovering flaws in the acquisition process that result in leakage of potential acquisitions.

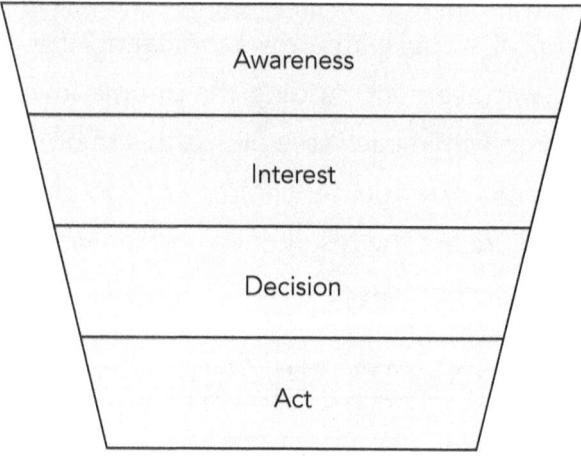

FRAMEWORK FOR EXTERNAL PROBLEMS

External problems refer to challenges inherent in the environment in which your organization operates. They represent external issues that your organization must respond to or overcome. While the origin of these issues is external, the frameworks used to identify possible solutions still require an internal component: a plan is only as good as your ability to execute it. Solutions that call for actions that are above your organizational capabilities, or require tools that your organization does not have access to are poor solutions.

There are many possible permutations of frameworks for an external Environment Analysis across numerous organizational contexts. A generic form of this analysis first breaks down the problem domain into the observable characteristics of the environment and your organization's sphere of influence. Within observable characteristics is another framework, developed by Harvard Business School professor Michael Porter in 1979 to analyze industry attractiveness. This framework is popularly known as Porter's Five Forces, and provides five distinct areas in which to analyze an environment.

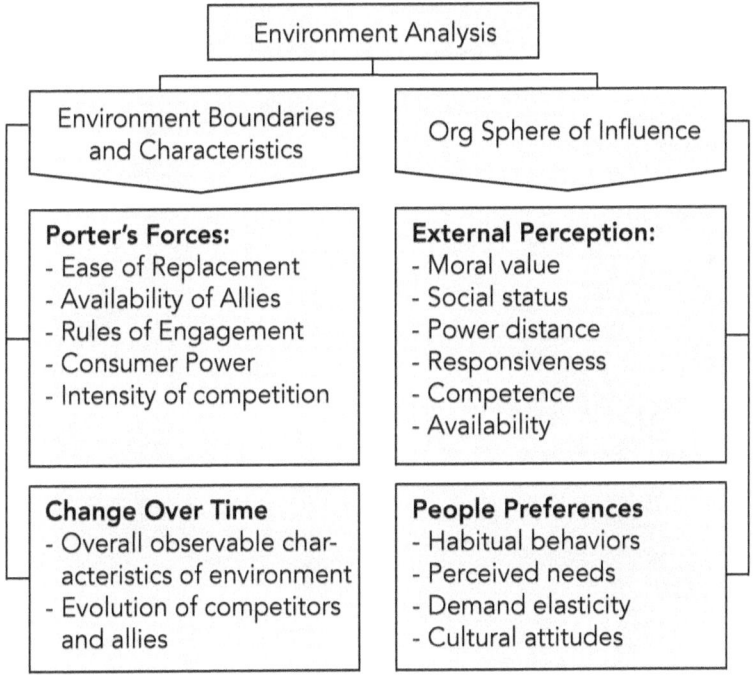

As the leader of an organization attempting to accomplish a strategic goal in a likely competitive environment, your most valuable tools are things that help you make better decisions faster than your opposition.

By flexibly tailoring exhaustive frameworks to the situations directly facing your organization, you can significantly decrease the time required to assess problems and take correct action. Over time, you also build cues to action based on a keen awareness of your operating environment and your organization's place within it.

Epilogue

It has never been easier for a person to create their own reality and build their own community within that reality. This book has catalogued the basic process through which an individual can accomplish this feat—starting first with self-awareness, then awareness of the people around them, and then, finally, awareness of human networks in which all of us exist. It is essential to avoid skipping steps in this process. While a lucky or well-positioned person can successfully build or co-opt networks to support their cause, that person will face a hard ceiling on what they can accomplish without also going down the path of mastering self-control or building empathy for others.

I deliberately avoided presenting my own normative views within this handbook. The most important reason is that the purpose of this book is to help the reader orient themselves towards a more strategic and less ideological view of human relations. This is not a book about what is wrong with the world or what should be done to fix it. The strategic view of the world is that it is dynamic, malleable, and does not inherently favor any particular value system or worldview. To some, this may seem exceedingly cold and calculated. We live in a world where power and influence are not distributed based on virtue, but based on mastery over the fictions that drive human behavior at the individual and societal level.

If there is one key takeaway from the principles covered in this handbook, it is to be imminently suspicious of normative arguments, appeals to rights, or an appeal to a supposed shared history. These are each the hallmark of an attempt to make you think ideologically, rather than strategically—to believe in a world in which options are constrained to a small orderly set of behaviors permitted by the speaker's worldview, rather than one that is chaotic and limitless.

A statement of ethical principles cannot be taken at face value. Invariably, it masks intentions that are purely self-interested. The greatest danger lies where that self-interest appears to actually coincide with yours. This is the point at which you are most vulnerable to being influenced and manipulated into exchanging capital (time, money, energy) in return for the promise of social rewards—rewards that will never come if there are others who have invested more than you have for the same rewards.

More than anything else, you are a free agent. This does not mean that there are no negative consequences in pursuing your own vision of the world; merely that any social or ethical constraints that you feel are a product of someone else imposing their own worldview onto you. There are no untouchable sacred cows, no shameful thoughts, no decisions that are off-limits. It is a burden, but also the best possible opportunity to create the world in which you wish to live.